The Light in the Film

The Light in the Film

Poems by

JORDAN SMITH

 UNIVERSITY OF TAMPA PRESS • TAMPA, FLORIDA

Manufactured in the United States of America
Printed on acid-free paper ∞
First Edition

The University of Tampa Press
401 West Kennedy Boulevard
Tampa, FL 33606

ISBN 978-1-59732-088-7 (hbk)
ISBN 978-1-59732-089-4 (pbk.)

Browse & order online at
http://utpress.ut.edu

Library of Congress Cataloging-in-Publication Data

Smith, Jordan.
    The light in the film : poems / by Jordan Smith. -- 1st ed.
        p. cm.
    ISBN 978-1-59732-088-7 (hbk : alk. paper) -- ISBN 978-1-59732-089-4 (pbk : alk. paper)
    I. Title.
    PS3569.M5375515L54 2011
    811'.54--dc22   2011022902

This book is in memory of Liam Rector

Contents

The Light in the Film

Cold Front

The young maple outside my window's contorting
In the wind. Oh, it's a dance—disfiguring and anguished
In the way of nature imitating art, which imitates
What we believe's our nature. I don't know. A tree
Grows resilience so it can suffer this, but suffering
Should have its ends, and this is juſt a change
In local weather: ſtorm warnings until noon, partial
Clearing then, a night's firſt froſt. Left to its own
Devices, a tree's a beautiful thing, not this riven
Splayed creature, and of course sympathy like this
Is recursive, sentimental. You know
What I'm going to say next. It's almoſt fall.

The Mind's

The mind's a flurry, Krishna says to Arjuna, hard
To rule. No net can hold it. And so the King
Nods to but cannot command his Earl—Wind-changing
Warwick—who might have been his good counselor,
Were the world unmade of all loyalty to mere division:
What's grasped from what's up for grabs. But in pure
Acquisitiveness there is no east nor west, revolving
Scimitar-like radius nor still center, only an encircling
Of troubled water around that almost broken Munch-like
Figure modernity has taught us to imagine as ourselves.
What I wanted, and this I hadn't known in my pursuit
Of happiness with credit card and mere devotion,
Seemed like an open hand: that all of want was there,
The emptiness of lack, desire's upswinging blankness,
And to choose between anything was no choice. Better
To simply bow. Oh, not to necessity, that bore at the bar
With an answer for everything, and not to defeat, his pale
Half-brother, hands scrunched in the pockets of a hand-me-down
Windbreaker, but to you who reads this, whose own wandering
Mind has led you this far, and why not, toward
Something you must have thought you wanted anyway.

Tile

Where once I wanted wood everywhere, floors
And cutting board, the currents of grain, isles of sapwood,
Polished, and the old oak library table pitted with use,
Speckled with spilled ink, now I am lost in the cool,
Reflected air of the tile store, a board of samples,
Rough to the touch, a kind of cuneiform water might write
On the creek's silt or wind on the sand cliffs of the park
Near my parents' house, places unreachable without
A sense that the ground was shifting under my feet,
That something was inscribed simply to show
How little words could tell of the world's immediacies.
So I'd like to make this choice with my eyes shut,
Forget the multiplicity of colors (even those beautiful ones
Patterned to look like kilims, permanent occasions
Of prayerfulness), forget the nostalgias of vision,
Where every drive leads to a home no longer there,
And imagine my fingers just touching the surface
Of one of those lakes named for the fingers,
Where my parents sailed, and, bored, I trailed my hand
Over the water, eyes closed, and the boat's motion
And the wave's were the same, seemed only a kind
Of interrupted stillness, and who wouldn't want
To have that back, a child's boredom where all of time's
In equilibrium between two shores, interminable,
And you can't even see the dock, not yet, not yet?
It doesn't matter if the tile is the blue-gray of the lake
Crested with whitecaps or the dark green of the vineyards
On the slopes, or the dun of the naked hill where the Senecas
Imagined a great serpent writhing. You can tell me
All the tales you want of the world's creation and its dull
Undoing. I'm here to look for stillness. I'm here.

[3]

Sonatina: Imaginary City

Like you, I live in an imaginary city, except mine
Might be Vienna, a place I've never been and am not
Likely to be, at twilight, always, late in the laſt century before
The laſt one, and there are lamps along the ſtreets, the sound
Of a celliſt tuning from a window, an artiſt's
Model pulling on her robe, since light and all else
Have failed to make the canvas anything but a botch
Of color better suited to the country, to yet another time,
Nature and God harmonizing before the sonata form
Began to seem moſtly artifice, juſt another means
To get something done that might almoſt not have been.
There are rooms warmed by coal, there are gaslights
In the foyer of the opera for a long evening of triſte
And Triſtan, there are sharp tangs of coffee and bitter
Chocolate from the cafes, but to imagine something is always
The opposite of possession, which is why I am outside,
Snow falling on my overcoat and hat, turning another
Corner and another. There is something I muſt do,
And each part muſt be done in order, one theme introduced,
Explained, and leading to another, but it muſt seem
As accidental as the viſta down one boulevard giving way
To the next. See, where that horse and cart recede
Into the diſtance which is not darkness, not exaċtly,
Although darkness is part of it, as the paſt is nothing,
Not a paradigm, not a respite, not a place of laſt resort,
Not even if you dwell on it, not even if you don't.

Consolation

I don't think reason is much. Try it on your lover
Who's depressed, I mean as clinical as that, just say
It's all in the synapses, which means all in the genes, which
Is all the higher reason we have, the biologist was saying
On the radio last night, a code like a computer's meant
To replicate according to plan, and anything else
Is the irrational number that will neither repeat nor end,
Which is the higher reason we want but can't follow.
So to say it's all repetition and variation is either to say
It's all art (never reason's friend) or to climb only far enough
Up the hill to the see forbidding spires on one hand, a great
Wilderness on the other, and know a logical life is spent
Neither here nor there nor there, but in some triangulation
Of options. And if I almost typed "neither hear nor their,"
Meaning, I guess, neither the pure immediacies of sound
Nor the possessive distances of things, that just goes
To show what can't be shown except in those narratives
That begin because someone isn't thinking clearly, makes
The misstep anyone would, and what follows is just proof
Of how little we have to offer in witness, in warning,
Except to say it follows, not knowing what might, what does.

On Hearing My Father Needs Another CT Scan

I sense a hollowness in the earth, and if, to be truthful,
It is not for the firſt time, ſtill there is a kind of permanence
Now in how my feet ſtrike a bell tone with each ſtep,
A breathy note with a dull and persiſtent core
Like a low whiſtle's slow movement of the slower air.
This earth you walk on with such contempt, a phrase
From the *Mahabhrata* — well, I have tried to leave
Behind all arrogance, and I have tried to forfeit and forget
The mereness of a grasping mind, but if this ground
Beneath my boots is loss and loss alone, the humus
No metaphor, but juſt particles of what's going, going,
Gone, then resentment seems the leaſt I can do, if not
The beſt I have to offer. He taught me to love Wagner's blaſt
Of brass and percussion, when Wotan ſtrikes the rock
With his ſtaff and summons Loge, god of fire's trans-
Mutations, but at the end, what's left of fire, what's
Left except a memory of sound's authority. Liſten
To the hollow earth resound, a call to the absence
Where something flickers towards vibration, flames away.

King Orfeo

And when he came it was gray stone,
Granite, with her features in the grain,
The skin of it he touched, her hair, which,
Graying, he had loved still more, yet
Felt nothing now, not even the well-
Deep coldness of ancient rock, long-
Cooled, its well-known indifference. Yes,
There was an echo, only that, of the fairy
World in the diminished scale he'd played
Since her vanishing, the flattened intervals
A passage into minutiae and decline
He followed, his thoughts of it a guttural
Almost song. And it was then that rock
Became portal, a threshold crossed even
As it appeared it might be. She was nowhere
To be seen, she was everywhere, slight thread
Of her red hair in a plaid woven of grays,
Dull heathers, where the hoofbeats were,
And no riders, then a company, lordly.
How had his pipes come into his hand
At their command? He touched the chanter's
Holes, knew the doubled, split reed's warbling
Grievance begin to sound a tune they all knew
Of failed, beautiful defiance,
                              The Hanged
Man's Reel, and she was there, not to return,
But to welcome him who had died with her,
He knew now, and how else to find out
He had this, just (exactly, only) this music in him.

I Still Can't Remember

. . . all the best things she said.

−Bob Dylan

If she appears in a dream's unrecognitions. If this
Is sleep's edge: twined ropes of her cloak's clasp.
If she has the half-familiarity of so much that goes
Unseen. If she steps from the exhaust, from the shadow
Of the concrete pillars in the hospital's ramp garage,
A shadow herself, of awe, of anxiety. If the sign
On the wall marks neither exit nor prayer, is a dim glyph,
Air-brushed by a desert's wind. If you have no one to blame
But yourself, the offerings neglected, invocations muttered
Half in mockery, the instruments of praise untuned.
If you heard the wind in the brittle limbs of pine
At the field's edge, and that brought you here. If you felt
Your head bow a little with the weight of her hand.
If that was almost enough, almost enough, almost too much,
Well, then we shall require of you a true account, without
Stammering or evasion, and then we shall ask again,
Even as you retreat in memory to where her vision
Began in your own blindness—that stone
You bent to pick up from the path, plain as day,
Its surface worn not quite smooth, the lines of quartz
You studied, thinking wrongly how little such intricate
Workings meant, thinking you could throw it away
As any god might this world, without loss or regret.

The Abstract Expressionist Has a Vision of Graves's White Goddess, 1954

Hung over, of course. But there was a woman walking.
He didn't know her, hadn't seen her or the three dogs
Flanking and circling her as she followed the crest where sand
Echoed the crest of the wave, where dimension failed
Not in flatness but in a shimmering of depth that was at once
The motion his heart made leaping toward her and the echo
Of what his brushstroke had seemed, her hair, only the echo of
The afternoon before, in the usual fury of the studio, where
His demons (a critic might say, given to cliché, who wouldn't
Know a devil if it jumped him in broad daylight, and certainly
Not his personal familiars, overly familiar, with their bad
Department store Midwestern suits and polite imprecations)
Had abandoned him for a half-dozen desperate collectors of the new,
Arriving early for the usual Friday night party, as bad or worse
As last week's, with their dog-eared *Reviews* and barometric sense
Of reputation's nuance. The dogs too were all line
And energy in a field that kept expanding as they dodged
From surf to tideline, but she whistled them back
From the coals of someone's beach fire, and he knew
She was just a neighbor from one of the summer places
A street or two closer to the shore than his. She turned
And watched (he saw it only as she did) a dark weight
Dragging lower in the deepening water, a seal's corpse,
And for some reason she raised her hands above her head,
Sand rippling from her fingers in the wind, and that was all
He needed to see to see past the next show and the next
To the great posthumous retrospective, when his work
Would already have entered the domain of nostalgia, but now,
Right now, he was as original as he was ever going to get.

Stones, Just Stones

for Judith Hall

Listen, my Druid friends, my neo-Pagans, undebauched
And unabashed by the modernist, skeptical irony
Learned by rote not heart, and of which even I've
Repented, but after such knowledge what was left but faith
In form, not spirit, and this is why I can tell you, and
Better late than never, that yes, there *are* spirits
In the wood, and no, they will not speak to us, or
Answer our conjectures, who have never left them
What they value most, that privacy which is the truth
Of myth, its life, its secret: that we were never meant
To see the nymphs of tree or spring, and if we did,
Such courtesy was required of us, to pretend we already
Knew that the observer alters the occasion, and so
There was nothing we could be certain of, and our prayers,
Our rites, might well be our slim best hope, but
As one word qualifies the promise of the next, we'd still
Be better off with stones, just stones, and nothing
Sacred about them, although how not to love the quartz
Patterning its spiral, its constellation in the red granite,
How not imagine a dance it seems to offer, to require
And follow, words and steps fainter, fainter, in the knowing
That no sacrifice is enough, anywhere near, to bring them back.

For the Fascists Who Worried

That art might be an incitement and a crime, not just
A diverting nuisance in the culture pages of the *Times*,
I'd like to say a few words. First, thanks (and I will,
As you'd insist, take care to avoid irony, proscribed
Always since it serves, as no one may, two masters,
Truth and folly, hand in hand) for the advice to keep
All sentences periodic, looseness of thought and dangling
Phrases being the hooks traitors are hoist upon,
Later. And thanks too, for that nostalgic glance, romantic,
Paradisiacal timelessness being the state's cure
When time hangs heavy on the powerful and prisoner
Alike, timeliness being left to the busy engineers,
Who understand it and need nothing else, and when
They do, they too can have the tickets to the opera,
The galleries of founder's portraits and landscapes
With ruins and sprites, all banished now, for good,
For our good, to nothing but fond remembrance.
And that is where I am off to this evening, with your
Blessing, an evening of sentimental and self-approving
Joy: the hero, oppressed in the first act by forces
He can neither resist nor comprehend, takes up his pen,
Writes a brilliant if slightly baroque *fantasie*, and by act three,
Is hosting a salon of the like-minded and ineffectual,
Opulent, claustrophobic, and from your point of view
Entirely benign. So, denatured, rarefied, and thoroughly
Bourgeois, our gratitude (and no, that clause is not misplaced),
Is yours, as are we, the undersigned who cannot write
A line but at your pleasure, your license, and our leisure.

Photography 101

On the subway, en route to Central Park, to shoot
The accidents of circumstance and physiognomy
That make a city worth the while of the connoisseur
Of the plain and the plain oddity, she said to her student
That each of the faces at the orgy the night before
Became more itself since the bodies were so
Interchangeable in their intercourse, and no part
Essential or irreplaceable, which made mortality easier
To take and less attractive, if saying so wasn't saying
The opposite of what she meant (she laughed) meaning
The *negative*, or, her student thought, some pun
About *contact* and *sheets*, that was, like her work, too
Obvious and too witty for easy viewing, because
Each face in all its distortions of makeup, wear
And tear, and plain (that word again!) bad feeling,
Was just itself, would never go beyond that, and mere
Judgment might as well undress now too, no room
For that pretense, you were either in the world or out,
And what you thought mattered, well, couldn't matter
Less than what you were willing to see, which wasn't
A matter of choice, simply, but of choosing, not
The possible, but the enacted. Take it from me,
She said, handing her student the camera bag, leaving
Only the old reflex dangling around her neck, you can't
Take more than one frame at click, and if that's not
Bad enough, you'll find that's all you have left of any
Moment you thought you might have more, and, hey,
Like the song says, that's no way to say goodbye.

Listening to Lew Welch Read Twelve Hermit Poems

You don't have to get it right much more than once,
And here this poor guy hits a dozen in a row, before
He walks into the mountains with his rifle and doesn't
Come back. Long ago, we'd have organized a search
Party, led by that trapper from Whitman's *Song* or Crane's
Indiana boy, with the prieſt who heard Berryman's laſt dreamy
Confession along for spiritual advice and moderniſt
Consolation, but now the country's too forbidding, the canyon
Narrows vision to a subway's labyrinth, fits and ſtarts,
And so I hit the replay button, following the thread
Of what's barely hoped for in that voice's wanderings, although
I can feel myself turning away too, onto a side path
That curls back down to the settlement, where the hearth
Is warming and the gossip deep, and none of this
Wandering seems necessary, since whenever someone ſtands,
Slips on the wool poncho and out the door, we can always
Recite another good hearsay odyssey and say *so long*.

The History of Rock & Roll

Is, sorry, banality, rising from the garage or art school, film
Studies or the store that sold the old Vocalion 78s,
Playing a big brother's left-over Kay or Stella, then
High school dances and a club way off the strip,
A wannabe booking-agent with a contract even worse
Than his taste. Then a few fans who follow the band
To the first real gigs, a song that isn't a cover
Of Robert Johnson or Petula Clark, and publishing
Rights given for nothing to the new manager, hipper
And a little vague, a little opaque at once . . .
Did I mention how the booze gives way to more
Refined experiments, about the same time the Fillmore
Offers an opening slot. And then the shared Victorian
House, then the ranch in the hills where the writing
Either kicks in or takes over, depending on whether you ask
The old groupies or the new ones. The personnel
Has changed of course, a mandala of bass players
And drummers, the songs are more *personal* someone
Tells an interviewer, which both explains and doesn't
How much anger is there on the stage, mike stands
Slammed and shirts ripped off, the security on edge
Even as the new up-and-coming guys tell the press
How washed-out and tie-dyed that old scene has become.
Whatever I've left out, it doesn't matter, the same
Old story coming back, like the opening scene of a movie
I watch over and over, the music, the helicopter blades, the fan
On the hotel ceiling right in synch when everything else is
Wrong, just wrong, and that's why we keep trying this old
Kid's game called *Break on Through*. And why we don't.

Idiom

He thought the local idioms were vanishing fast
Enough without his help, which is why he stood,
Hands in the pockets of his hunter's check jacket
Outside the convenience store at the triangle
Of three roads leading nowhere he had any business
To go, and couldn't make up his mind. His coffee
Steamed in the cup resting on the car's hood; the dog
Looked up, curious but patient from the passenger
Side. He was somewhere between Saugerties and
Woodstock, somewhere between the ordinary and the mythic,
And any moment the houses, maybe that plain old
Pink and white one where he'd turned around when the road
Ended, or almost, in a farm lane, ought to resonate
With meaning or memory or . . . But he was a tourist,
Is all, he thought, without guidebook or portfolio
Of any old times, much less the good ones, and that tree
Where the old state road veered off in gravel, the tree
Shaped like a devil's fork on some horror flick poster
Or album cover—well, was it a warning not to go
Much farther, or just his old, habitual timidity
Showing its other face? There was a diner he'd passed,
Next to a clutch of trailers, and maybe it was time
To sit for awhile, listen to how they talked around here,
His own voice, but a little different, the way you can drive
A long way to get nowhere fast when that's the whole
Idea, or say everything while not saying much at all.

The Brief Sadness of the Baroque

First the instruments themselves became more beautiful—
The simplest line of the flute putting on the turned
Rings of ivory, the chromatic foppery of a single key,
The violin becoming less merely sensuous, less gut and sinew,
More a scroll's literary elaborations—transgressions, really,
Like a major-domo's minor revelations or a relative waiting,
Unexpectedly, at the door through which tumbrels are heard,
Or at least the conniving whispers of the lower servants.
That the evening is so beautiful is the burden of the counter-
Tenor's song; it cannot last. What's past (the recorder's
Descant yielding to something persistent in the lower strings)
Is past grasping. And the prospect, so pleasing by daylight through
These arched windows, is at night all reflection, all
Decoration, flare of candles, and the powdered wigs bowing,
Except that to shape such detail, such triviality of attention,
Requires an iron of intent, like the turner's chisel, which
Is also his knowledge, held like resentment against the turning
World, knowing how much, for this brief beauty, must be
Pared away.

Ives

The fifer practices in the belfry, until the tolling
Begins, and, oh, what hand has turned the bells to play
Their call to meeting now? It's not joyful, exactly—
This is New England, after all—is predicated
On a strictness of intent and slight release, but
There's humor in the timing, the fifer just ending
Soldier's Joy when the bell's *Doxology* begins
And the fire department band, the one I played in
For free beer and five bucks a night, rounds the corner
And into the trio of *The Stars and Stripes Forever*,
And what could be better? It's not in how badly we play,
As if centuries of practice couldn't make a democracy
Out of late imperial defensiveness, and it's not just
The juxtaposition of man, and god, and law, but
You had to be there the fifer might say, ears still ringing,
Climbing down the belfry stairs, mouthing those words
About *fifteen-cent morphine* and *twenty-five-cent beer*,
And laughing as he joins in with the passing piccolos,
Off-rhyming *forever* with *get me out of here*.

Treason

In the old days, treason was the lord's hand, a weighty
Deity on the shoulder, a blessing to be shrugged off in search
Of a better. *My vassal.* My lord. And later, it was a queſtion, not
Of loyalty, but of a merchant's candor, who beſt will feed
My pretty wife, my conſtantly dwindling accounts, and such
A man might well take revenge at being passed over
Despite his merits, since merit should be all, should be
Rewarded. And later ſtill, the arrogant ideologues, a refined,
A vintage diſtaſte for the ordinary life of partial detachment,
When betrayal, when hatred could fuel such cold fire.
But always it was the undoing of words. Language
Was a currency, no more, and secrets survived only
In their passing, from mouth to hand to gloved hand, to
An unexpeſted vanishing, a might-have-been becoming
A never. So treason remained always a quiet trade,
Well-suited to its old disciplines—refusal, greed, and pride—
As to its disciples, servants of civility, inconspicuous,
And all the more so, if powerful: those who will not serve
Except in the hell they'd make for the reſt of us, living
In the usual way, in some belief or in its undoing, whichever
Made us feel more loyal to what we had, without
Much hope maybe, but (what saved us) without contempt.

Nantucket Reds

The man wearing washed-red khakis sits at the surf's edge,
With the red setter gallivanting around him in the sweet
Flow of tide and early sunrise, as if the world was newly
Created just for them, and no one else sits watching
In a car so old it still takes leaded gas, smells of Kent
Menthols, with a couple of short, thick casting rods
And a bait bucket on the torn back seat. So it all depends
On where you're sitting if this is or isn't an ordinary
Morning, as even the familiar bitterness of coffee
Depends on how you brew it, and the lineage
Of the beans, and who you think you are, drinking
For a sharp and self-approving pleasure or just
To wake the hell up. As for me, friends, I'm neither
Here nor there, not on the rocks of the breakwater
With a portable radio tuned to the oldies station
And a quarter can of last night's beer, and not by the bay
Window of that shingled and artistically weathered house
With the deck facing the dunes, an empty cup on the table,
A dog's bowl underneath. If I seem to be everywhere
And nowhere in this landscape, well, it's just what I wanted
To believe: that a myth of origins might include more than a day
Of rest, a real vacation, but then that demiurge showed up, the one
Who actually makes things, and I thought, well, better
Tell the truth, better plug the internet back in and turn on
The phone again, unless you can really afford everything
You desire, and without even the thinnest edge of a knife's
Taste for irony, get it, get it by all means, by any means at all.

The Light in the Film

That light in the film last night, the one about a girl
In the low-rent suburbs going off the rails, and each scene
With a blue or greenish cast, not natural, but still
The way it looks, exactly, when you know what you know
Is more than you should and less than you need to, which
Is how it feels to me most days, when I've no need
For that jittery, hand-held camera work to remind me
That the national drug is caffeine and for good reason (we
Just can't catch up). It left me sleepless, that film,
Thinking about walking around my neighborhood and how
Unsettlingly quiet the streets could seem, everyone somewhere
Else, so I almost missed the old muscle cars, the Furies,
The motorheads used to drive, the hot-rodded exhausts and jacked
Rear ends, since that's when the country seemed most itself,
Menace channeled into machinery and momentum, and maybe
The cost of a service economy and all those closed factories
And our habitual violence exported wholesale, is just this
Stillness, the bad light coming back, and the hurt, hurtful
Face of a girl too young for that handful of pills and razor
blades, except she's not taking them, friend, she's offering
To share, to fix the score and every broken piece.

Egypt

That's the town's name, like Ovid, Mycenae,
Sodom, even—that's what happens when the auto-
Didacts settle the place, sacred texts in hand, and barely
A thought to what's under foot, these glacial fieldstones,
Say, tumbled like fallen obelisks, glyphs scratched
Down their faces, that he's gathering in the wheelbarrow
For the garden wall, a folly, pure symbol, but what
Might last as long? The Greek Revival house he bought
In the '60s, gutted out and replastered, everything done
The old way, or as much as the building code allowed,
After the divorce, after he left teaching to set up
As a craftsman, the lathe and chisels in the old barn
A woodstove warmed, after the classes in meditation
And sacred movement—all these *afters*, and never
A glimmer of what might come next. It's all hills here,
Not much sun gets through so late in autumn,
Beyond the shop and fallow orchard, although the little
Mansions are rising there now, and the mall traffic,
And there is something dispiriting about the turner's
Work, all that whittling away, the pile of chips for the fire,
In the service of what?—form, he thinks, the shape
The wood was meant to take, but how often has he sanded,
Patched and painted, finally replaced the fluted porch
Pillars? He has a pair of rough work gloves, a checked
Wool shirt. He looks, he thinks, like any local, before
Local meant nothing lasting, and he has decided
On a monument that hardly anyone will notice, so
Anonymous that when it falls, it will still show the maker's
Hand, the cold and implacable grinding of stone on stone
The earth sets off by simply turning, turning until
Nothing is left except what's never enough.

A Chinese Landscape

You can see it from the road between Poland and Russia,
New York, a gathering of those camel's-hump hills
Where a monk might live a lifetime on rice, meditation,
And once in a while a Genny Twelve Horse Ale and a slab
Of rat cheese, and write poems terser than this one,
Since knowledge hardly needs words. If I could draw,
I'd praise those shapes—as elemental, as uncanny
As the Maine woods that made Thoreau cry out
Who are we, where are we?—with just a few lines,
Sharp and suggestive at once, and if I could sing, well,
I'd find a banjo-tuned mountain ballad to take all
Loneliness into a few broken high notes, but no,
I can't, and so the landscape is a simple rebuke, and
Yes, I acknowledge my insufficiency in the face of matter
Shaped so grandly. But what I do understand
Is how they got that way, that narrative of persistence
And erosion that, like story-tellers in a circle, each
Of us can tell only part of, the part we know best, and
Have figured out least, and here's mine: along Route 29,
Someone has painted just the front of a barn, the roof
Already sloping hard toward the south, and just one door
Of the rusting-out truck behind it, and if you look hard
You'll see him wipe his hands on his jeans, toss
The brush uncleaned onto the bench, and walk toward
Lunch or a beer or whatever you do when you've done enough.

Another State

Why do I think there must be an answer in another State,
Connecticut, say, where Ives and Stevens labored to ensure
The diversity of the senses and of reason should never
Go unrewarded, nor smallness of mind unadmonished, even
The believer's, even the unbeliever's, who walk the same
Road from their white Federal or Greek Revival houses
To the Congregational Church, where the organist has pulled
The trumpet and piccolo stops, and slipped a few bars
Of Liberty into the baroque offertory, just a little nudge in our ribs
Or God's, whichever handle you take it by. And outside,
The sky is somewhere between Impressionist pleasure and Modernist
Suspicion that it's all a con, and then the house again, the door
Opening on the antiquities that remind a young country
That tradition's one thing, but you might always need another—
Privilege, say, meaning the imagination's self-sufficiency,
Which is where I'd like to live, but can't begin to find myself,
Thinking of all the little towns that line the roads between here
And the State line. First the route climbs through a woods
Where half the turnoff signs say Old State Highway and loop back
A mile from where they began, then a descent, a few trailers, a frame
House, a crossroads with a cycle shop, convenience store, what's left
Of a lumber yard, then garage sales, and even as the road climbs
I can't find that Emersonian vantage, although only a few miles
Away, one man saw a river billowing from nothing to his vision,
And another married Harmony and called her name in ways
We might all recognize and still never have imagined.

The Transcendental Set: 3 Reels

1. The Dedication to Mt. Greylock

If the world is everything that might be, and yet not
Everything we might desire, well, then a man writing
An unfinishably brave book might want a mountain
Looming there on the horizon, a name like a cipher,
A face like a glyph, and an approach trail, rich
In mud after these spring rains, so he can imagine
The picnic party of Transcendentalists in search of what
Sublimity might be on offer, slipping from slick
Rock to Berkshire slop, and each step pulled free, like
The stylus of a Sumerian scribe from the tablet, which
For all its antiquity, is the cuneiform of mere transaction,
Grain for wine or slaves for blood. No epic there.
You might as well read a whaler's logbook, and he laughs
As if a rogue sunbeam on the mountain's rock had lit
For just a moment a little outcrop of sandstone,
A fossil caught there, some few and splendid bones,
Some great fish weighted in the grayscale of it all.

2. The Transcendental Band

A good band ſtarts a little before the beat, the drawn
Breath, cocked wriſt behind the bow, and something you'd
Hardly see if you were looking, and they don't have to,
Not quite a nod, but ſtill a geſture of assent, all the reel
Requires.

3. The Orchid

Too sleepy to keep the tune going, I ſtop, look up, and there's
The orchid's bloom—ſtippled, loopily symmetrical, over-
Refined—too much so to suggeſt intelligence. It muſt
Be will (or some wonderful implosion of it) designed
Such elegance paſt mere funƈtion. Orchids, greyhounds,
The flute's grain of wood and sound, this particular shade
Of evening, of noſtalgia. Oh, diminished light, unfinished
Tunes, unvarnished sentiments of dark and oiled wood, made
Bright in focus . . . You have been called, the orchid says,
To such attendance, as the greyhound's sleekness drives
The lure, as the flute's smooth weight in your hands
Asks for breath. Breathe, I told myself, but of course
I hadn't ſtopped, except as you might ſtop to begin again.

Contradance

. . . the children they wouldn't have had otherwise.
                                    —Norman Dubie

The grange hall's white bleached wood walls,
Like whalebone, and outside sleet
Has begun to pile up on the windshields
Of their cars, dancers who've driven here from Troy
And Ovid and Mycenae, from Liberty
And Industry and other towns of myth and duty,
Some with kids in tow, some with fiddles
Under their arms, and they've made a pile of wool coats
And instrument cases in one corner, and two lines
Of dancers and a third of musicians who are going wildly
Out of tune as the wood stove flares, playing
A set from even further north, of old-time wedding reels,
And the women and the men bowing, partner
To partner, have been doing this a long time, moving
Through the world hand to hand, staving off the weather
With whatever fuel there is and a little fire,
Keeping the kids from burning themselves, and themselves
A little warm, not too much, because you don't want to forget
That cold, even as the sweat breaks from a long spin
Up and down the rough floorboards, and you're back now
In the arms of the one that brought you, hand on that arm
Through all the thick wool of the sweater—the muscle,
The changes; the eyes you look into, right now . . . you don't
Want to forget that's why you came.

Do Nothing, Know Nothing

When the eye of Reason opens . . .

Causes and spirits appear, or almost, if nothing can appear
As nothing must, as insubstantial as the mind that wakes
To its own insubstantiality. And it takes a trivial mind
To ask that permanence be existence's test, even in high
Summer when the trees are so present, the grass, the rising
Thunderheads that I can only imagine more by the image
Of a Shaker-like *less*. On the table, a still life of baseball cap,
Coffee mug, notebook, flute, and the eye renders each
Transparent, malleable in the frame of vision, which excludes
As easily as it takes in, which is why the visionary seems,
Or only seems, as beside the point as someone else's
Apocryphal *Apocalypse According to* . . . you'd probably
Have to be there, or expect to be. But the cap is stained
Around the brim, the notebook half full, the wood around
The tone holes of the flute has darkened with each note,
With the opacity of things touched and used, each more
Distinct then with each instance of its presence. So, given
A choice between the eye's transparency and Thoreau's
Jury-rigged playhouse by a pond, I'd take the sills worn
From an elbow's leisure any day and every, although
He only stayed there a little while, although the bent nails
They found in the cellar home were as good a poem as this.

American Studies

for John Irwin

They're almoſt passé—the old boys, Thoreau and Emerson
And grim, gray Hawthorne, who made my life this dream-
State I prefer, that transcendentally obscure bank
Of clouds I can juſt see through gaps in the oak trees
This late summer night, the edges lit by fireworks
From the town park, the delayed celebration of a rained-
Out Fourth. From that half-dark basement seminar room
A few miles from where Poe traded his vote for drink
To this suburban backyard, I'd like to think I'd kept
Faith with the glimpse of madness at what words (those
Poor illusioniſts with such a low threshold of intoxication)
Can say about what the mind can do and about the world
The mind can only conjure, a flicker like a mis-shot rocket, a flag
Of flares, those sparklers we ran around with on the slope
Of my grandfather's lawn that ended with a sand-cliff
At the edge of one of those lakes we call great because
They seem to lead to no other shore. So all we've got
Is what we have, which means we have to invent it.
All of it, although we never know (it goes so faſt, a lit match,
Sparks and powder and the hissing, snaking splendor's
Warning: *don't tread on me*) what to do with the insubſtantial
Except make light of it, make words of it, make do.

American Studies, Again

I slept on the couch in Matthiessen's study at Harvard,
Twenty-odd years ago, a guest after a reading, and there
On the shelves, the first editions of the writers he knew,
And in the room that chilly silence I'd always associated
With being somewhere I didn't truly belong, not
Unwelcome, exactly, but not entitled either, and that's
The shame of democracy, a friend told me once, we
Have to accept what we do not love, which is never the same
As loving what we would prefer not to accept, and so
Whitman wrote only a *Paradiso*, and left the rest of us
The purgatory of knowing how far we might fall, even
With good intentions and all our sentiments intact,
Though affection is something else again, a kind of distance
Erased by love, not will. Will builds the ordered
Quadrangle I walked to get here, lays the subway rails
And tiles the stations, and that is where I stood the next
Morning with kit bag and manuscript and pen, and nothing
To write in that tunnel, until I saw two lovers leaning
Together, as if all quarrels were over, and the news-
Paper they shared, circling ads in the classifieds, had been
Printed out of sheer sympathy for what they needed,
As if we all might agree to get along to go along, a little
While, at least, wherever and whomever that meant.

On His Unbelief

It's boring, this modernity, this no-exit strategy,
Of which my teacher once accused me, no believer
Himself, but he knew the easy way when he saw it,
Having refused it so often, and he was tired, I think,
By then of helping beginners with their little
Variations on the ego and its (nothing but) discontents.
Caustic, sarcastic, is what he said, with that good ear
For the off-rhyme, and walked off, leaving me to apologies
And correspondences, the making of metaphors, one
After the other, for the nothing I professed.
With my portfolio of x'd-out likenesses, my degree
Zero of authority. I thought I'd learned just about
All I could about how language unsettles everything,
Which meant I could say *sorry* or *so what* in a dozen differing
Voices and never, as they say, mean anything by it,
And never offend or disappoint, except myself, because I knew
Another story of tongues, how on Pentecost they burst
Into flame, and speech became a common splendor anyone
Might grasp, who knew no more than could be unknown,
And that's more than me, who never listened half enough.

Coffee & Free Association

—for Peter Heinegg

There's self-indulgence and then there's self-
Indulgence, meaning you've paid already for whatever
Forgiveness you'll be needing after you've said
What you had to say. And if you believe that,
I mean even a little, you're back where you started;
Since knowledge is not a deal struck, a conditional tenure,
With the garrulous Gods of Right Speech, it's not
A *daimon* or gift, something you're born with, and die,
Unlucky, with less of (think Crane, think Kerouac,
Those supervisors of bridges and roads, and other
Modes of exit). No, it's a trick of slight but certainly
Inevitable and observable motion, coffee and free
Association, and in a few moments (few enough,
Never enough), there's a chorus, *sotto voce*, praising
A brilliance in the air, not yours and just enough
To see by, for those who can, and who indulge themselves
In sight, and never the others, who've taken the text,
Nailed it to the door, and shuffled gladly away, pleased
With the devil on their shoulder and all the trouble
They'll be causing you when you've said what they know,
(because you told them), they just knew you had to say.

Master of None

The absence of disciples is notable; although cushions
And rugs litter the floor and light ricochets from pale-
Paneled wall to pale-paneled wall, the room is as empty
As the mind should be, of all desire for flattery, of all
Flattery, of all desire. *Shouldn't*, his own mantra
Might remind him, *shouldn't silence be enough*, but
Always he had a gloss to offer, a flood light bringing out
The singular blush in the flower he held aloft, an hour
Of commentary on a gesture meant to contain no time,
No time at all. Once when he talked, they came
To listen, the pilgrims with their soft-soled shoes,
The spiritual incorrigibles, books and shoulder bags
And visas stamped at Auroville or Findhorn, and always
They had as much to say as to hear. *You know the story
Of Babel*, he asked them finally, seated in the Hall
Of Competing Interpretations, *you know how simple
All that destruction was. The sun became a mirror,
And the mirror a prism, such fragments of adoration,
Which are our words, but there is no syntax now, no
Common* . . . And he found, then, he had nothing more to say.

Dead Letter

I could sleep for a thousand years . . .
                                    –Lou Reed

Like O'Hara said, you could write a poem instead of picking up
The phone, and the poem, typed on a yellow second sheet,
Jammed in an envelope, stamped, sent off, but with the wrong
Address. A dead letter, but not as lost as the body on a stretcher
Those friends are straining to lift in the painting, into darkness
And farther. In the silver-papered loft, the guitarist tunes
Or untunes the strings; he wants that dissonance, just the right
Indeterminate space between the notes of the chords, simple
Repeated chords, and nothing simple, the right estrangement
Of the ordinary from the ordinary self's ordinary estrangement.
The song's a whip, a bow slipping from the hand of the cellist
Who cannot stand to receive the applause she's earned—but that's
Nothing to him, to you or to me, except that the stories we tell
Tell us how far we might go to get farther, those hours of practice
And that sense of impartial, inconsequential failure, against
The mere in mere mortality. A solution, then, just one solution
Among all those other ways of construing the world. So,
Is this why I'm happy, listening to songs of desperation
Rewarded or at least affirmed, although I'm driving to work,
Although my interest in transgression, like my job, is mostly
Academic, although I've got no voice and couldn't care less whatever
Might drive *you* beyond all assumptions, all categories, not even this
Envy I'm not feeling, because if I did, well, then I would.

Tosca in Mexico

That it is impossible, of course, that she survived the fall
From the wall of the Castel Sant'Angelo, does not mean
It is unimaginable. She was a shard, after the execution
Of her lover, one of those fragments saved for all
They imply of art and the story behind it, the story which
Is always of a vessel broken, and a shard dropped
From a great height is still a shard at the end. So, perhaps,
A small miracle, that she should land on a cart of straw
Driven by a peasant who loved both a voice's beauty
And liberty, and so her travels would begin, clandestine
At first, and finally, after the mud, the terrible roads,
The illness aboard ship, the awful bartering for passage,
She would awaken here, an edge of desert, a dry river
And a house that might dissolve in any heavy rain,
And a landscape telling her only and exactly what she knew.
In the next house, a potter, throwing crude bowls
On a cruder wheel, and singing as he worked just the few
Same notes, over and over, and she had to hear it
For weeks before she recognized the fifth bar of the aria
She sang to such acclaim before the leaders of the new
Republic and would have sung to their Bourbon captors too,
Since art has either no master or however many are to hand,
Which, she would have said, amounts to the same thing. But now
Recognizing those notes which came just before the modulation
From order to dissonance, and hearing the talk in the café
Of rebellion, she knew the dust in her throat was meant
To quiet her at last, and limping, she walked the road to town
To see where a knife might be purchased, if that's what was needed
  now.

Purcell, in Hell

Someone muſt write the table music for the feaſt
Of loſt souls, cymbals to rattle as brazenly
As the empty plates set there and a consort
Of viols to make the gut ſtrings sing out as if
Freshly torn, so bright the sound, and so sorrowful
The silences which are not reſts, each a pause merely
Before the lamentation recommences, as if
To consider praise and rejeƈt it as trivial,
As sycophantic. We know how Job was loſt
To whim, God and the Adversary like two schoolboys
At a bet, so if a composer's needed, why not
Call in a few divine favors, so much business between
The Capitals being done with a nod, a wink, a flick
Of the tail. So Henry Purcell, that gifted psalmodiſt
Of church and banquet hall (*welcome to all*
The pleasures that delight of ev'ry sense the grateful
Appetite) muſt descend to this, another work
For the theatre. It promises the exotic, soon
It will draw Mozart and Berlioz to draw demons to their nibs,
But this is a bluff and hearty Englishman, whose
Pleasure is simply that, and so the ſtage set is ordinary,
A line of tables, a roaſting beaſt, good wine and better
Beer, and the countertenor's voice lifting in impossible
Longing, while those who will never be fed, having taſted
Their fill and more, ſtand about with the ſtricken looks
Of a party whose reservation has been loſt, and he,
The composer of each quaver of joy they cannot have,
Has ſtuffed a bottle in one capacious coat pocket, a loaf
In another, as if this earthly food were reward enough, so
Sing, and why not, *come, ye sons of art, away.*

Brunch with Orpheus and Persephone

They are the travelers snowbound in the first class lounge
Whose reservations for Park City must have been mislaid,
Whose delayed flight means, oh, not another night
In the corporate suite, although what job they might do
For their money is as unclear as why they might need
To do *anything*. A little past their prime, but still
An eyeful for any tourist's cell phone camera, and if
Some sweet singer of songs comes on the muzak, well,
You can be sure *he's* mouthing the words, and if the *Vanity
Fair* open on her lap has a new spread of second-generation
Hollywood ingénues, you might see her wince, but
Immortality has that price—to never change, although
The world does and thinks you do, there at the telescope's
Far, wrong end. He might pick up another gig, well,
Locally, and she might tantrum and bluff her way
To a free meal, fruit and cereal at least, waiting for their
Revised itinerary, through Taos or anywhere with the shortest
Layover. And for the rest of us, Mormons or Maenads,
We can hum along to his greatest hit—was it *Waiting
For the Sun?*—the one he dedicated to her to get
Something else he wanted and wouldn't let himself keep.
We can play it over and over, and say we saw them once,
Stuck, just like us, and just as real as it gets.

Yes, Wagner; Yes, Again

That scene where Alberich whispers to Hagen, *mein sohn*,
And neither you nor he can tell it from dream, as who
Doesn't have a father's voice like that, insistent—no
Not a true father and not a Father of Lies, that easy
Manichean digression, but somewhere between the two,
That voice with its program music, it's assertion that the world
Is one way only, and to listen is to become it, in detail,
In design, is to have designs on it like etchings
On a mirror. I'm groggy, waking from this afternoon nap;
I'm tired of the world as I find it, so there's the temptation,
To shrug, just shrug, and sleep some more. And yet,
Somewhere in the linden light beyond the porch, a hero
Steals back the gift he was given and gave away,
And who will set such license right, the voice is asking, and hardly
Knowing what I mean I nod, assenting, waking as if inside
The voice, the dream, which, as Freud instructs, is work,
To bring to light . . .
                        No, it is a darkness this voice would recall,
Blood shade on the underside of a leaf's blade even in summer,
How any splendor makes you cover your eyes, and that dusk
That is the cupped hand held there, and if you follow
Those branched lines back to their source, you'll hear it:
Help me my son, and know you might as well be lost
Here at the start of it all, whose undoing you meant,
And meant to be, and were meant to be, at first, at last.

Sky, More Sky

Early winter sky so grey all day it might be twilight
All day, and yet I told myself I'd learn to love it, nothing
Less, and come to it like a brother approaching another
Brother in the mirror, with likeness and unlikeliness
Reversed in that double portrait. But it's no accident
We gave the gods the clouds in which to dwell and raise
Their havoc, their monuments to war and love's
Compulsion, since neither their glory of sun nor their
Twilight are ours to share; like us, they mirror themselves
Alone, and neither understand nor are to be understood.
I'd like to think the conditions of my life are more
Than *whether*, more than choice's accident, but what's worse
Would be some intention sheer as the wind buffeted
Between shifting clouds and ground. Who can be appeased?
Not the weather-maker, the old sad self; surely not
The lord of whatever, barging in on the virgin or the old couple
In the myth, not the hero, that happy home-wrecker.
There's an oak tree in the yard with a splitting trunk, and no one
Knows why the bark curls away over a scabby eye
Of wood, but look there long enough you'll see the clouds'
Reflection and your own, and wonder, not so much how
Or why, but if there were anything to those old stories
Where wisdom rose from the earth, and we couldn't find our tongues.

Snow Sky, Backward Glance

Forget the whole Orphean hymnal, the sonnets
And books of changes, the Gnostic chants, and metaphor's
Metamorphoses. Forget the steps they taught you,
Widdershins or crane-footed, the alphabet of trees
Against a horizon, mist lit by new sun. It's too dark
Now to read, four in the afternoon, a snow sky out the westward
Kitchen window, Bob Dylan on the stereo, don't
Look back, that old advice, still good. It's another northeastern
Pastoral, dead of winter, a squall coming in, which is how
I always thought I'd go at last, a walk into thickening snow
Past the little lights of a suburban street, each
A halo of no particular meaning, since no house
Was the right house. Well, I like the quiet well enough,
But also this backward glance through a stack of old albums
And books I've held onto since high school, words
To live by, which is what I did, I see now, with gratitude
However much I fumbled around the edges, however much
I didn't get it right, style or substance, I don't think I missed
Many chances, at least not to listen to what the songs meant
But never said, not exactly, since it can't be said because who
Knows if you don't, right now, the only time there is.

Sentiment

Pra&ticing tonight, the usual fumbled intricacies of jigs and reels,
All speed and ornament, those modern insi&tences, as if tradition,
Memory having failed, required at lea&t good hand-eye coordination
And a metronome . . . And then I fell into a waltz, which is
Like falling asleep near a hedge of the sweet primroses in some
Old ballad; the territory is enchanted, enthorned, enthroned, and
    keeps
Its own time, and unbelievers are unwelcome, the faithful put
To the te&t of transformation, whose only proof is love. Was I
Found wanting, or only re&tless, wanting to move on to the next
Tune and the next, one only a little different from the other, in ways
I hardly heard, laboring to get the rolls and triplets, cuts and &trikes
    in place.
It's like learning a language I had never really heard, and then,
Fru&trated and sleepy, I found a few notes and then a few more
Of one of those old songs I hardly knew I knew—*Oft In the Stilly Night*
Or *Believe Me If All Those Endearing Young Charms*—that come
So swiftly back, it's like the embarrassment of an emotion you're too
Young to feel: sitting in the dark of my grandmother's front parlor,
Leafing through the book on the piano's music &tand, hearing
One 78 or another crackling toward pure &tatic on the old
    phonograph,
But underneath, some voice that once was fine, and some sentiment
That couldn't be finer in the face of what no child knows is coming.
And she was in the kitchen, singing along. And then, the &tatic
At the end of things, I mean as she mu&t have seen it, before
We reinvented the world as decoration added to decoration,
    without
Finding what we'd lo&t, what rose amid&t the brambles and was
    gone.

Reunion

The fireplace is twelve feet wide, a great millstone set in brick
Above the hearth, as if it were a child's pinwheel heat might turn,
And my mother, eighty-nine this year, sits below that suspended,
Implacable weight, her face lit, although no fire's laid. It's mid-
Summer. I haven't seen her look like this since I was a child,
And I'm not the only one to notice: *You're lovely*, one of the cousins-
In-law says, *I want you to touch me before you leave, so I
Can take that beauty with me.* Well, if truth is strange because
I take so much of it for granted, then it takes a stranger to tell it
True, I guess. Earlier, I'd watched her sister watch the window
For my parents' car, watch and watch, and then her face too
Blazed as they pulled in. At the pool table, the young
Almost-cousins take turns at a game they've made up,
Of spheres, trajectories, and objects spinning in space, as long
As objects last in space, energy and inertia. *That's beauty,*
Someone says, or I think they do in the pleasant, drowsy
Swell and flow of talk, *the orderly, the ordinary, always
About to vanish.* There's a lake, I'd like to think, just down
The hill, and a canoe there, gliding, and this island that is
No island, since nothing is as separate as it might seem, not
The night, now, and our bodies at speech and at rest, not
The moonlight's sweet waltz on the water I can't see from here,
Though I can see enough of bright and dark to know that nothing,
I think nothing, rubs off on us like beauty as we row home.

From the Notebook

The tempter said: look, I can read your poems over
Your shoulder, and it's like you've learned nothing
I could teach you. I said: I know who you are. And he:
You do, and you don't. Let me tell you, friendly advice.
No more rereading Thomas Mann. No more scribbling
In the magic margins, pacts with no one, hallucinations
Offering excellence at the price of an audience. No
More Wagner on the ſtereo, no more *zauber*, flute
Or mountain, no more sentiment of loſt whatever. I said:
OK, but you're not promising anything. He said:
Would you believe me if I did? That's how it works:
The *via negativa*: you give up everything, or at leaſt
All the glamour of things, and in return. Yes:
I said. He said: No. If I'd explained it right,
You'd never agree. Not duſt, not fire, not wind, not
Even that. Yes, I said: You see how badly I want to sleep.

The Flute is Zero

The flute is a zero, cusp of nothing, and then
The void was troubled, they say, a turbulence,
As if God sighed at how much work was to be done,
Not creation—we all love that—but all that maintenance,
And the sigh became a whistle, nonchalant,
Like Whitman, loafing with his hands and all the universe
In his pockets, and in the empty circle emptiness
Was amplified and shapely, resonant, till pitch
Joined frequency, and fingers altered flow
To song, and practice made, if nothing perfect,
At least a tune you could recall, whistle, maybe
Dance to, although all dancing is a kind of stumbling
After one good reason after another not to simply,
Better, stay still, better contemplate the void, but we
Have found that one foot forward, one foot back
Marks time and erases it, plus and minus, equals
Zero, anyway, but sounds like so much more.

Extra Beats Per Minute

The cardiologist said the tachycardia was a sign
Of nothing at all, but what's the use of talking
Like that? I'd seen the spikes on the EKG's
Graph, and what was I trained for if not to read
Between the lines any moving finger writes,
Even that spindly, digital beckoner. There it goes
Again, that syncopation, and if I love the way
A good fiddler pushes the first note of the repeats
Just a little ahead, still there are places I'd rather
Not get in any hurry, thanks. So, driving home
From the ER, I thought that God's text, this leaf-
Struck suburb, was more burnished than usual
From possibility or sudden revision, all
Those finite meanings repeated like a mantra,
Each natural fact singing out it's corresponding
Spiritual one, and so loud and with such frequency
It all seemed a kind of glissandoing *hum*. Say it,
I said to myself, almost laughing, *hum*, and only
Just in time switched on the tape to save myself
From that self-approving vortex, better off
With another set of reels. Sure, they all sound alike,
Which only means the possibilities of variation
Are endless, pushing that beat forward, and who
Wouldn't doubt that he might not prefer
The next one, the next one, and the one after that.

An Episode, an Event

They called it an episode, they called it an event,
As if it were narrative, as if it were spectacle, her first
Embolism and then the second, a week later, but mostly
It was waiting for the nothing we hoped would happen,
In the ER, in the cubicles, and the in the ward,
A week's worth, with an ex-nurse in the other bed
Who'd smoked too long, asked again for more meds,
Because she knew what she wanted, tried again
To rip off the oxygen mask. And the first thing
I gave up was narrative, since who wanted the ending
Circumstances implied, and the second was witness, since
There was so much I didn't think I could afford to see.
It was only sound I waited for, footsteps in the hall
Meaning they were bringing more pills, or
That the doctor with the Russian accent had another
Question to ask, answer not to give, story to tell
About how his father died just this way, and all
I wanted for the next big event anyway was a remake
Of a story we'd all but forgotten, some ordinary day.

As Needed

Xanax, 1 mg, as needed, which is up to me,
I guess, who needs or doesn't that cold white
Flower at the brain's Stem. And what am I trading:
Skeptical irony for spiking adrenalin, even, a wash,
I think, when I talk to my wife in the hospital
After her second pulmonary embolism in two weekends.
Oh, I was clearer-headed than that winter's day, as sharp,
As numb, knowing the road to the ER, the routine
Of triage and waiting, good at pretending it wasn't,
Nothing was happening. Are *you* taking care,
The good wishers all ask, and *yes* I say, meaning
I've got my mechanisms of defense all in place,
Got one foot moving ahead of the next, and
That's all folks, until the pills wear off, and what's
Left is what I Started with, minus whatever this new
Need is I've learned, now that I know what's needed.

After Reading Transtromer

I don't think I have been writing with enough tenderness.
If I had, would the snow ſtill be falling? Ah, it is an old
Ruthlessness filling the visitor's lot at the hospital, sending
The car fishtailing across the interseĉtion, an old greed
To crown everything with silence, as I said nothing
To the woman who lay so easily, so noisily near death
Next to my wife in the recovery room, where they let me in
Out of pity, I had been waiting so long, and I was speechless
With relief to tell the two apart. You see, there is no
Tenderness in silence, nor in speech that does nothing
To comfort, to mend, but bows in resignation, a man
In too light a jacket, shivering, walking to his car
In the almoſt empty parking lot where it juſt goes on snowing.

Herbal

If cilantro is for gender, that insinuating musk
Of brokenness, of longing, then oregano is the sun
Of the troubadours, light annealed in a blade,
Oiled, drawn from a scented sheath. If chives
Are the bite of the ordinary, lush and common,
Serious in their rank insistence, then sage is the logic
Of addition and basil the wisdom of slow distillation,
Of the mortar's dankness, the pestle's labor. If garlic
Is the fruit of our labors, then our labors surrender
In flowering what passes for pleasure. If tarragon
And lavender are taste's eccentricity, then rosemary
Is its antidote to parsimony and parsley its commonplace.
If drying preserves the cumin's rankness, and oil
The pepper's bite and rancor, and vinegar its savor, then
Even if the margins of the herbalist's journal are thumbed
To a fine dust, it will be the dust of the sidewalk
Outside the old spice factory (cumin, coriander, dill)
In Baltimore, even after a night's drinking, the scent
Like powder slipping from the spoon in someone's
Loving, measured hand. Remember the song
On the jukebox in that bar? If it was true, then
There is and will be always something there to remind me.
Then the book of herbs is simply another leaf in the great
Volume of correspondences, and who could have written
Better and with greater economy of the various scents
Emptiness takes, sweet and poignant, there and not.

[49]

Art Song

–for Liam Rector

This old inn, supposedly haunted, with its drawing room
Of Victorian brick & brack, its acanthus-leaved plaster, and neat
Half-ring of chairs around the piano would be the perfect
Place for the recital I've planned of all my omitted sins.
That's art, you see, that's song—not *I'll tell my tale*
As though 'were none of mine, but its mere mirror's
Silver lining: I didn't do anything (no blame), but desire
Knows all guilt's pleasure of saying exactly what I did
Not. You see, I studied with the great monologists, the silent ones
Whose gestures simply continued behind the scrims
When the talkies came in, becoming all nuance, a dialogue
Of shadows that more colorful confessions hardly illuminate.
But it was illumination that came to me, in a room
Like this one, a little intimidating, a little too elegant,
A place, in other words, to which I might aspire, and if
I lied right away, sang like a canary, to talk my way in,
Well I was hardly the first false witness to bear and get better
Than I gave, measure for measure: between the bar lines,
These black flecks of melody a voice might join and join,
Or the mirror of a voice. That's art, like I said,
Sprechstimme, that's song, almost, different from life, and better
And not, and longer. As long as it is wrong.

Rather More Baroque

Rather more baroque than not, this life I'm examining, pleased
Enough at how pattern defeats design, memory's eye, glancing
Off one variation after another, then the inversion, recapitulating,
Mostly, now, its own quiet splendors of movement, and that
Seems the most of it, going through these motions, only to find
How little can be repeated exactly, if only because
It repeats, and that's the principle and privilege of memory—
A kind of aristocracy, offering patronage to the self that actually
Did all that work, selecting out the weak, wheat from the chaff,
And riffraff, a connoisseurship whose theme is whatever it takes
The theme to be. And yet, how cranky even the most pampered
Dependent can be. The artist, having painted the face of the prince
Disguised in *The Marriage at Cana*, begins his sketch after
The Gnostic heresies; the same potentate is now a grotesque
Demiurge, and he hides it in the score of the composer
Who shares his study, interleaved with the cantata whose notes
Encode a parody of the dinner-time praise song or a lament
For the passing of a poor, almost unnoticed supernumerary,
His wife. So memory unselects at best, and here I am, thinking
What was the muse was never anything but an intricacy
That admits nothing, that survives retelling as nothing
But elegance, should we believe that part of everyone's design.

Speaking in Tongues

First of all you have to experience that power
Of interruption, how the desire to speak displaces
Speech. There's a tension below the jaw, as if
Something clenched in air, and the mouth begins
To learn what's asked, to answer what can't be;
The eye, startled, starts, and the nerves' reticulations
Find expression in a net of impulse and mis-
Firing, which has its own logic, no longer self-
And-other, but some nested parenthetical, the tongue
Curtailed and fluttering, the ear's labyrinth of curls
And feedback. Neither ignorance nor understanding
Is the least help, nor the studs and piercings meant
To appease or embarrass mere desire, nor the gag
And hood of conscience or conscious deception. This
Is the gift ungiven, the frame-by-frame undoing
Of time and time's intent, and the I of love eyeing
A world that stands between it and the world,
Where speech is passport, map, and all direction
Home's a stumbling now in darkness, and all
The echoes you can handle, and more to come.

The Second Look

—for Ruth Stevenson

The pattern in the Persian carpet that becomes
A skull at second glance is where you might
Begin this recognition that each trip through
The text recalls the one before, as a drive
From Wellfleet to Truro recalls a road map
From the Thirties as your beſt and only guide
To what Hopper saw that you might see. Rereading
The poem in progress, I've caught three typos
And a solecism, a word that suggeſts so much more
Than mere error, some fundamental disconneĉtion
If the weft of things where nothing seems coherent
Except by rule, and the rules as arbitrary as the choice,
Right or left, at an unmarked crossroads, no devil
In sight to play let's make a deal and set your hands
To the slide and ſtrings. I meant to ſtart
With the Renaissance, so it should be a lute, not
Robert Johnson's small-bodied Gibson, but let's
Retrace the ſteps: the figure of a skull hidden
In a rug, *momento mori*, the songs of Dowland
And Campion, of love—tell me then how the littleſt
Of deaths, as unrepeatable as the grandeſt, becomes
Another madonna and child or a song that laſts
Centuries out, so no surprise when the player shuffles
I Saw My Lady Weepe up againſt *Devil's Got My Woman*
Juſt as I drive paſt an old relic of a single-pump
Gas ſtation. How many times have I seen it before,
Juſt not quite this way, which moved me ask you,
You know what I like about Marlowe? He knew
Hell was everywhere and all in the repetition, and he didn't
Need to say it more than once. Since you should know.

It's Not Over Until It Starts Over

– for Ed Pavlic

As Johnny Cash sings, *I got it one piece at a time,*
Which doesn't mean I don't ſtill get mixed up
Between autodidaĉts and automatic writers—
Not the willful, surrealiſt undoing of the will, but
The spirit mediums, whose hands move to some
Diĉtation of otherness, or other. On one side,
The weedy paths of Concord, a border of sage
Next to a field of rye, and a pond glittering
Brighteſt when framed through an awkwardly-
Carpentered, unglazed window. You make
What you will of it, since they did. And on the other,
The Fox Siſters; *you remember,* they say,
Rapping out the message of their decade; *all
The loſt details of the ones you loſt,* and that's
As much them now as the deareſt notions
Of the dearly departed they summoned back
From parlor tricks and transcendental musings,
Hardly more misleading than a hermit's visits
Home for dinner, waiting while his washing's done.
And if it's all a sleight of hand—genial or ingenuous or
Engendering—then what does it matter exaĉtly
When we caught on or how long we didn't, as
Driving my good old '68 Rambler American, I might
Point out how much pop-riveted sheet metal and epoxy
I ſtuck on there, juſt to keep the whole thing going,
Or I might not, since what would it matter, so long
As we found our way deeper into that sun-ſtuck glare,
Nowhere in particular or juſt plain nowhere.

Country

– for David Rigsbee

I knew I was in trouble when I stopped listening
To the country stations the radio's scan picked up
On the drive from Little Falls to Victor, the valley
Of the shadow of nothing in Central New York,
Where the hills had voices once, where prophets
Rose in Palmyra and Oneida, and maybe even here,
In a diner near the Herkimer exit, someone
Brooding over a cup of bad coffee will get up,
Drive to the scrubby margin of his farm, and hear
A command, a revelation, that has nothing,
Nothing at all, to do with the bank or the government,
And his speech will be wild, yes, but only until
We really listen. I shouldn't be thinking this way,
I thought, the tires humming like prayer wheels
On the thruway, turn the radio back on, listen
To some sad song about what people do to each other.
But that was the problem, you see, I was driving home
Where someone was dying, and that was no one's
Fault at all, and nothing in the world could fix it,
So what good were stories about what anyone meant
To do or didn't, sorrow with blame attached.
If a visitation of angels can shake you, a leaf's
Aurora in early autumn, long past, then how much worse
The anticipation of nothing at all, a sort of howling
Like wind rushing past a car's cracked window.
I could use a good tune about anything, I knew,
Dim lights, or smoke, or loud music, anything
But the steady glare from the almost iced-up trees.

Empty Racetrack, Early Morning

Empty, except for a single horse crossing between
The grandstand and the barns, the rider in shorts
And a sweatshirt, the thoroughbred's lanky pace,
Long lines. You'd like to think *Degas*, you'd like
To think what it's like here in summer, the silks
Of the jockeys, the crowd, straw hats and sun-
Dresses, but it is almost fall, this is practice, not
Perfection, not the sudden break from the pack,
The lengthening beauty of a stride, that long shot
Coming home. This is what you do in a fallen
World, a controlled trot around the barren enclosure,
Hoofs striking the scarlet of downed maple leaves,
Feeling for a halt in the gait, a muscle's reluctance,
Injury's insistence, something to be worked out.
What else was the curse when the garden gate
Closed, but this careful labor to make right what's
Not and never will be. Oh, if it is love, it is not
Something nuanced, fine, and selfless (or more
Than the less the self is). It is the love of a parent,
Desperate, for the wrong child, the one drifting in the wind
Of his very own distracted discontent, the one we couldn't
Save, not exactly, any more than we could ourselves.

Student Running in Fog

She's barely there, at the fog's lead edge, the bulk
Of the gilded-age mansions off campus almost lost behind her.
Running in sweats and cap briefly into focus, as if history
Receded just so from her stride on the sidewalk, and envy—
Who's to envy what no one can see? The weather's
Densest where she rounds the intersection towards the stables.
Is this all possibility or all foreclosure, I asked the real
Estate agent over coffee, meaning not the mist, not exactly
The floating mortgage she was offering, not to me, speaking
Hardly even hypothetically, but to anyone who'd take an interest
In anchoring a piece of this unmoored world, but her answer
Was like a series of quickening steps along a beach, the tide
Rising, no point in looking back at what's no longer there.
Yes, I thought, that's just what it's like to be so young,
So fleet, following the slight upgrade in the sidewalk
Like the graph of consumer confidence on the business page,
Hardly aware of the gravity, the exertion, the crack a sloppily
Placed foot might catch on. I had work to get to, the pattern
Of a day in the agenda, which would hardly be different from
The last, the next, or so I had every reason to hope, and hope
The one good reason, the best consolation, at last and at least.

How to Get to My Temporary Office

—for Matthew Graham

The mansions on North Broadway are the real thing. An hour's
Walking tour and you'd barely begin the survey of the anatomy
And taxonomy of the crenellations of the chimneys, the history
Of the forms leisure takes, brick by brick, from the hands
Of those less so. You'd need the time to study it, which is why
The speed limit is low, but the traffic's expected to keep moving;
A slow trawl past these blocks is what the neighborhood watch
Is watching for. The point is to be impressed and go home,
Since this is a tourist economy, and transience is a virtue
I share, teaching as a visitor, enjoying the facades without much
Reference to the interiors; it's as comfortable as an unopened
Volume of James on the nightstand. To get here, like my friend said,
Could take five minutes or as many generations of immigrant
Striving and unbelievable luck, and it's just mine
To be heading to work after breakfast on a fine fall day, and forget
Until the last quick turn that I need to hit the bank for money
And one coffee shop or another, so why not park downtown
And walk the rest of the way. Well, you know that feeling
Of being a guest at the country club: someone's signing
The chit for the drinks and someone else has the wine list
Well in hand, but as soon as the talk turns to politics . . .
When I took my kids to Hyde Park and the Roosevelts's charming
Old-deal house, I saw all the antique furniture my parents had saved,
Upstairs where the servants lived. That's the anecdote
I pull out at times like this, hoping to show a little class, but
You'd be surprised how no one gets it, or maybe not
At how polite the silence after is.

The Blind Harper

My road lies in darkness . . .
—Charlie Musselwhite

The epic ends badly, the hero so at a loss in the gauzy
Gray meshes of an inadequately realized underworld,
That even the bull-maned monster might seem a poor
Simulacrum, lurching, lopsided, from the maker's failure
To imagine, if not a way through, at least a sign of forgiveness.
At least a ripple in the fabric of things, suggesting an off-
Stage fan, a spirit exterior to all this absence, even
Of longing, even of pity for the poor soul traveling there.
Still, there is such single-mindedness about it, all
Those lines repeating themselves, the hands fumbling across the
Scrim in every direction, it is hard not believe how the first
Audience must have sat, in a trance of anticipation, hearing
The notes between the notes in that recitation, which
Was neither mode nor its exclusion; what's heartbreak
Without some possibility? It's easy enough to dismiss—
Metaphor, and not the best, a fragment noted in the canon's
Margins for historical interest and good intentions—but I
Thought I understood as I looked up why I'd never understood
The blues, the eternal repetition of those three chords,
The way the notes bend from pitch. You have to believe there's no
Way out but out, and go there, step by halved by quartered step.

Unlikely Places

I was looking for the ſtables on the outskirts
Of the campus, for a place to reſt in the pace and gloss
Of privilege, to ſtand awhile, hands in pockets,
Like Whitman, amused and self-sufficient, but turned
Right wrongly, and then there were a few frame bungalows
Hardly painted since the '30s, and then the edge of town
You've heard so much about in song and ſtory, but
No darkness here, only the moſt gradual shading off
Toward afternoon above an autumn field of drying
Queen Anne's Lace and milkweed. It was like, well,
It *was* walking into diminishment. And then, a dream—
You know the kind—the dream that leads to the moſt
Unlikely places: firſt a small path, barely a rabbit run,
Then a road that shouldn't be here at all, going nowhere
Faſt: a ſtand of locuſts and a few fishermen's shacks
By the river's edge where I thought no river ran, a sudden
Chill. Well, it was early November, and night coming on
With November's haſte, and this was the sort of place
You see on TV, the place where the bodies are found,
Because no one would think to look for them anywhere else.
I'd been walking a long way to come here, left sympathy
Like an old friend who leaned back againſt a fence rail
And waved me ahead towards a shanty door, cracked open,
Leaves drifted on a threshold where no two might walk abreaſt.

The Dream of the Wheel

Not fate's, in the lady's hand, and not the great
Mandala of gods and demons, not Kerouac's *wheel*
Of the quivering meat conception, nor Pinsky's figurations, nor some
Other praise of radical continuities, but bright, unblemished,
Honed to an edge of utter impersonality, a sort
Of reverse god, whose circumference was everywhere,
Whose center, unimaginable point of zero friction,
Was hope's nowhere, was the end of Dante's funnel,
Was also everywhere. I'd been dreaming of my family,
Parents and children, after a long evening's vigil
Waiting for the snow to start, a nor'easter's revolving
Progression up the weather radar, after an afternoon
Stocking gas for the car and food, and there it was
In the gloved hands of the guy at the deli, the wheel
Slicing as thin as I cared it to what I needed to live.

Liberty

–for Peg Boyers

That black dog, large and into everything. That bounder,
Nose at work, scrabbling and scratching, stalking
The larder, scenting the boundaries, begging for affection
Then stretching the leash taut. Well-named, an idea
Of freedom at the tether's end, and if it breaks, call, call,
See at whose whim she returns. See *if* she returns.
It's July. The neighbors have hoisted their flag:
Don't Tread on Me. The evening will be fireworks
On the horizon or this storm that's building, building
Hemming and hawing, like an old-fashioned turntable,
The arm skipping and repeating in the groove, a few
Notes of Sousa, trumpets and piccolos and trombones
Threatening a melody they can't play yet. The dog
Is sitting near the closed gate of the stockade fence,
And she barks, waiting. There's a half-empty beer bottle
On the porch table, condensation on the long neck,
So much humidity, and everything is still, still.
The liberty we meant to have, we all meant to have,
Is waiting, wagging a tail, ready to leap, and *down*,
We say, *down, stay,* as if the only impediments were our
Generosity as masters, our endless self-restraint.
But that black dog is restless, chafing, wriggling, and either
She hears the thunder we can't yet, or she doesn't.
And, yes, she'd follow us anywhere, as long
As she wanted to and we had food in our hands.

Class Analysis

–for Hugh Jenkins

It begins in sin, they say, the simple act of greed
Become defiance, become the expulsion from love
And the curse to labor, and who wants to be cursed,
Would not spend all he has to get more without
The trouble of bringing forth anything. So, class,
I might begin, we divide the work from the worker,
The worker from the profit, which, like all surplus,
Is just what's left of what we imagine love's original
Fullness might have been, but really I fall silent before
I get to that last point, having gone from descriptive
Reason into the pathos that is theology, or at least
That's mine. And anyway, they still believe
They'll get that job, the one that reconciles need
With what we give up in its name. Sure, I was broke
A good long time, then barely getting by, and now,
I can't tell them, it's easier but no different. We're
Reading a book about a war where for a few moments
Love and anarchy and work were one joyful, exploding
Moment, but how could that happen, except in war's
Paradise of immediacy, where it looked like there was no
Better choice. But choice comes back, that old division
Into more or less, and then you're on your own, my friend,
Marching with the ones like you against the ones
That aren't, but, really, who knew which side you were on,
Until the waiter came with the bill, and you either
Paid it or went back to the kitchen to help wash up,
And either way you thought it might get better, by and by.

Two Poems for Donald Justice

1. I Was Trying Today

I was trying today not to think about music,
Not to be taken in again. Not by the breathy mortality
Of the flute, protesting its endlessness, until you hear
That pause, that quick gasp of air. Not the piano's promise
Of steadiness, of fixed pitch and solid temperament.
A few flurries, then something between mist and snow.
And I honestly don't know if it was the view out the kitchen window
Or the poem I was reading, a supple, quiet line, so brief
That still seemed to leave nothing out, nothing
Of the moment at least, but it was like a tune you play
And keep repeating, though it never seems the same
The next time through. I might have been walking in the pine woods
With no plan to go home, the dog loping ahead, looking
Just over her shoulder to see if I still followed.
I might have been lost (and I was) in some ordinary
Premonition of sorrow.

2. The Room Above

The only light in a block of flats, minor ſtrain
Of evening, as if someone loſt the keys
And can't imagine leaving home, not even
To look for them, now that the park
Is dark and the busses, almoſt empty,
Run later, later. But he can't reſt
Either as loss is casual, simple, and not
Final unless he decides it is, switches
The lamp off, sleeps or not. A loose door
Bangs as the wind kicks in, and a newspaper
Scrapes along the sidewalk, one of those
Free weeklies he might pick up and drop again,
Even with an ad he's circled, something
He guessed might be retrievable in all this flux
Of junk, then he put it on the bench, keys
On top, and walked away. So when darkness
Finally covered the face of this building, I wrote
That maybe he'd jimmied the door, and now,
He was ſtill awake, waiting, breath held,
For dawn's good old creation, but, you know,
There was something I couldn't place
About him, and this is it.

One More Take on My Funny Valentine

He doesn't know what they're thinking, not
The sax man in some sort of a deep brood
Through two choruses of I Just Can't Get Started, not
The thin guy on bass with the fixed stare, the drummer
As crisp as that accountant in Heart of Darkness
On the snare, the leader with his shades, ducktail,
Trumpet locked in a heavyweight's clinch.
He's just as dapper as they are, tweed jacket and tie,
At his table near the front, a good glass of scotch,
Carefully paced, and when they've done a few fast ones,
Got the house in their hands, and now, almost
Ex nihilo, the slow ballad begins, well, he's done
With the drink, too polite to signal the waitress, now
That the first few breathy trumpet notes signal
That anticipation of the lonely. He'd like
To be their brother in the dream this music gives him,
He'd like Audrey Hepburn, all gamin and good
Intentions to walk into the club and over to him,
But he hardly even knows what he's thinking,
Following the bass on the slow stroll through the changes,
The drum telling him just how late it is for this
Little bit of sad desire, and the sax nods once
At the trumpet, a little gracious, a little dismissive,
And his solo tells you everything you'd want to know
About why you don't know a thing they're telling you.

Classical Elegy

The ancients abhorred ease, she might have said,
That's why all those declensions. You can't say it right
Without . . . Declining, I would have answered; trying
To get it right, to avoid the obvious, is to slip
On language's slope. And what about Socrates,
That poser of the unanswerable, who banished the poets
For daring to believe in appearances without believing
That's all there is. Even Alcibiades might have taught him,
Love of the beautiful is only half the game. The rest
Is stumbling, drunk, on the descent from Apollo's temple,
Mud caking your soles. Think of Achilles in Dis,
Mourning not eternity, but phenomena, the mirror
Of blood where he appeared resolving, untroubled now,
Into a blur, a still life . . . but still, life. So, that last
Undoing in a foggy valley is no mere poet's *setting*:
It's the discipline of makers, of making do, not
Seeing through. *So you're neither seeing through it,*
Nor seeing it through, she'd have found the wit to say,
Fond of the last and oldest words, my friend who died today.

For His Biographer

Of course you'll want to interview me, the minor character
In the *bildungsroman*, the one whose insights across an otherwise
Unenchanted evening in a crowded room or through the stillness
Above the seminar table, will lend *a point of view*, or so
Your letter said, *to the mere details*. And yes, I'm your man,
Too self-effacing to point out that the details *are* the mirror
When breath dissolves, and familiar, too, with the relevant texts,
Primary (his poems, his poems) and secondary, those model
Lives—Orwell, and Lowell, and Crane, and Montgomery Clift,
(But no, scratch Berryman, scratch Jarrell, off-rhymes and snappy
Sport coats and all, since there was no late conversion and no
Ambiguity of circumstance). I've got stories and some quietly
Devotional rhetoric, if that's what you're after, and I was there
When certain things were said or not, and I can tell you who
To trust and just how far we'll all, all of us who knew him,
Go to lie on his behalf or our own (far, not far enough).
I'm ready to talk, but you might want to hurry. No, it's not
Memory that's going. But if time's short, so is patience;
That was his lesson. So listen carefully. I won't want to repeat
Too often that none of this matters except that he had a notebook
With him always, back then, blue cloth and maroon leather, like
An old-fashioned ledger, and what he wrote down there stayed
With me, and stays like that old expression: *he put paid to*, ending
On a preposition, as if something were coming, were coming, were only
Delayed.

How I Failed

How I failed you, my friend: first, by my reticence,
Which was also resistance, which was a way
That was no way at all towards the truth, if truth
Was final, was silence, was the rest after speech
Tires of its insufficiency. Then there was the mirror
I offered only for its silver, the quicksilver, never
The image, but its mutability. And of course,
I read you badly, taking the literal for the figurative,
The fugitive, and letting escape what I did not
Wish to know. And even now, I will not say
Well, if I knew then what I know now, because
I don't, and that should be the last example, since
It was the last mistake as well: to mistake a principle
For an instance, the whole for the part, tenor for vehicle.
You loved those old English roadsters which offered
A few hours magnificence tooling around Vermont
For days bloodying knuckles under the hood, and
If I thought that was an aesthetic, not a way of life, still
It's how I'd prefer to remember you: in your good jacket,
Leaning with a smoke against the fast little car, better
And more elegant than another pun on corpse and *corpus*, better
Than another workshop session turning into another exposition
Of my failure to understand that you always, always
Meant exactly what you said. Well, chalk it up
To an education that mistook *close reading* for a way
Of closing a door and getting on with it, which, I think
You'd just as soon I did, if, as you did, you had your way.

Chairs

My friend said he'd like to die in a leather wing chair
In the library of the alumnae club of his laſt and beſt-
Known university, chortling into his brandy over some obit
In the *Times*, and of course I thought this was juſt
Another of his unsettling parodies, parables of what we might
Have been, if not for the world's (more or less) benevolent
Intrusions. But he took matters into his own hands, sooner
Rather than later, and in a way neither parody nor irony
Could explain away, and I was left with the image of a chair,
A body's imprint there, like that crummy green swivel thing
In my office, the one I never bothered to replace, because
It was too much trouble, because *never* was a concept
I declined to entertain, although, poor hoſt, I greeted
Students and other junior versions of the self I'd thought
I meant to be, when it seems all I wanted was to be left alone
To read. And what? His books, maybe, as familiar and as
Uncomfortable as a habitual seat in the library of that club
Where nobody really wanted in, but here we are.

August

The elegy is what I cannot say.
Not emotion recollected in what tranquility,
Not filtered through the repression that is my locus,
A house almost paid off, walls, framed prints,
The quiet book I am reading about the unquiet nineteenth century,
That antique writing chest the appraiser said was an officer's,
Probably in the Civil War, and no one knows how it came to us.
My friend who killed himself, what was the stuggle he lost?
He was always of two minds, like a great nation must be
For ambition to flourish and to be checked by radical kindness.
If I want to think of peace, I think of a line of Federal houses.
That's how self-deceiving I can be. The bricked
Streets the troops marched through in summer heat,
Campaign season. The planning behind the doors.

So Long, Visionary Company

I thought at first I heard a hand drum's rhythm, a heartbeat
Under the fingers' trance on the keyboard, as if negotiation
Were possible between repetition and conclusion—
A cliché, of course, sex, death, Freud, and what else to expect
After all those books, Lawrence and Miller and friends
Lounging in the Whitmanian green room, waiting
Backstage for a curtain call that isn't coming, *waiting*
For the end, boys . . . Repeat it often enough, repeat
Anything and it will seem true, then not, or not as much.
So wanting ecstasy in the face of mere stupid apocalypse
(not now, but soon enough), meant wanting a moment
Out of time, meant trial and error, so many books, so
Few readers, since they, after all, had their own hands
To play before it all folded up the big tent and slipped away.
And what seemed a drum was just the misfiring pistons
Of a carny truck pulling for another town of suckers, nothing
Primitive and holy, no shaman rising toward the smoke-
Hole, since you know and I know, we all know, wishful thinking
When we hear it. But hear this, friends: I've been through
That broken sky, I've risen like a cloud over an uninspected
Power plant, and I'm back again to say enough's enough,
And so is any kind of glimmer, glimpse, or gloss that tells
You how lucky you are, yes, despite, because and even, even so.

The Veil

Not Salome's, which muſt have hidden something worth
Seeing, or else why so much dancing around the point,
So much exegesis, and not of the body only, surely,
That simple crucifixion of simple faĉts, but *hers*, a miracle,
If deadly, if impetuous and adolescent, which muſt be seen
To be believed. And then dismissed, juſt another bit of late
Bourgeois consumption in an empire fraying badly
At the edges like a country club Persian carpet. No,
I was thinking, if thinking is the word, of how difficult it is
To speak without modeſty, if modeſty is the word for that veil
Of language, which never reveals all it could because
It can't. See, here in Lucien Freud's catalog, a whole
Shopping liſt of flesh's imperfeĉtions: the privileged of the earth
Take off their clothes, drowse or ſtare, and it is not pretty
The way flesh sags into repose, the way sleep hones the fear
Of what it beſt mimics. It is not pretty, the way my words
Grasp and covet and cover their tracks, because, oh yes,
If the dancer and the dance are as insufferable as they are
Inseparable, it is only that we see them as Herod saw
His own worſt intentions, barely veiled, as if the sufferings
Of desire were any excuse at all, as if his command (*Dance,*
Salome) were whim, as if he didn't get exaĉtly what he asked.

Luck

I'm driving a decent car, listening to Greg Brown
Of Iowa, sing about a place he's almost given up on,
And where I used to live, and in that past tense is all
I know of luck: that I could forget the crummy apartment
On South Lucas Street with the crumbling stucco
And the punk rock coming through the ceiling, although
Mornings, on the public radio station, they read best-
Sellers, in which the poorer got richer, and love too.
And why did I listen, if not for the luxury of an extra
Hour before classes and a dumb (unspoken, that is,
Unspeakable) belief that things might turn out well, or well
Enough. And they did, more or less, but that's the forked
End of the wrong stick, as if accounts could be balanced
Moment to moment, as if *it hasn't happened yet*
Guaranteed it wouldn't or might not, or luck just might
Never run out. Ah, luck, which unlike memory, is never
Subject to unchallenged proof, makes no promises, takes
No bribes, at least not seriously, and leaves us, because
We imagined her so, lady of the wheel and karmic
Bookkeeper, random generator of effects nobody caused,
With only one question: whether it is better to slip by her
Unseen, or stare into those slot-machine eyes, when really
It's a coin toss, and anyone could tell that this is what
She does, since it's what she does: she shrugs.

False Positives

The photo teacher said my son's negatives were too
Thin, not enough *visual information*, and here are the x-rays,
Loaded, over-determined, and thankfully wrong, and both
Propose a reader who can tell sufficiency from the least
Or most of things. So I, who never pray except
In the stupidest fear, suddenly think that this is the problem:
I've only imagined a god who listens and judges, not
A *reader* who interprets, finds things to his liking or not,
Closes the book to get the phone, or falls asleep, or drinks another
Coffee over second thoughts, and all the while the plot goes on for
    him
Like one of those dreams I never have, the ones you can change,
The ones you believe in even though you know you're dreaming.
Listen, I could say in a dream like that, I'm talking
To you, and it would be up to me if you were or weren't
There, if you'd paid attention to the substance and style
Which is all I might mean, in the dream, by *me*, synecdoche
For all I don't understand. I thought I understood
What the doctor had to say, but he was, wrong, it turned out,
And so was I, happily back in the thin mystery of it all.

Notes

I Still Can't Remember. Title and epigraph from *Isis*, by Bob Dylan and Jacques Levy, copyright 1975,1985 Ram's Horn Music.

Photography 101. Hey, That's No Way to Say Goodbye, Leonard Cohen, Stranger Music Inc., BMI. Details from *Diane Arbus: A Biography*, by Patricia Bosworth, W.W. Norton, 2005.

Contradance. Epigraph from Norman Dubie's *The Alehouse Sonnets*, Pitt Poetry Series, 1971.

It's Not Over Until It Starts Over. I got it one piece at a time, from the song by Wayne Kemp, recorded by Johnny Cash, 1975.

The Blind Harper. The epigraph is from "My Road Lies in Darkness" by Charlie Musselwhite, recorded on his album *Sanctuary*, World Music, 2004.

Dead Letter. Epigraph from *Venus in Furs* by Lou Reed, recorded on *The Velvet Underground and Nico*, Verve, 1967.

Speaking in Tongues: After photographs by Liam Smith.

The Dream of the Wheel. Jack Kerouac's phrase, "the wheel of the quivering meat conception" is from *Mexico City Blues: 242 Choruses*, Grove Press, 1994.

So Long Visionary Company. The phrase "Waiting for the end, boys" is William Empson's, but I am remembering it from the title of an essay in John Berryman's *The Freedom of the Poet* (New York: Farrar, Straus & Giroux, 1976).

Acknowledgments

Some of these poems appeared in print or online in *Agni*, *Right Hand Pointing*, *Smartish Pace*, *Two Review*, *Western Humanities Review*, and *The Yale Review*, and are reprinted here with thanks to the editors. A selection of the poems was included in the online chapbook, *The Flute is Zero*, published by Right Hand Pointing and edited by Dale Wisely.

About the Author

Jordan Smith is the author of *The Names of Things Are Leaving* University of Tampa Press, 2005) and *For Appearances* (University of Tampa Press, 2002), first winner of the Tampa Review Prize for Poetry. His other books include *An Apology for Loving the Old Hymns* (Princeton University Press, 1982), *Lucky Seven* (Wesleyan University Press, 1988), *The Household of Continuance* (Copper Beech Press, 1992), and *Three Grange Halls*, which was co-winner of the 2002 chapbook award from Swan Scythe Press. His poems have appeared in *Antaeus, The Paris Review, Poetry, The Woodstock Journal, The Yale Review, New England Review, DoubleTake, The Cortland Review, Salmagundi*, and others. His work has been supported by grants from the John Simon Guggenheim Foundation, the National Endowment for the Arts, the Ingram Merrill Foundation, and the New York State Council for the Arts. Since 1981, he has taught at Union College. He lives in eastern New York with his wife Malie and their three sons.

About the Book

The Light in the Film is set in Deepdene types designed in 1927 by Frederic Goudy and named for his home and studio in Marlboro, New York, where he designed it, only about ninety miles from where Jordan Smith and his family now reside. Goudy cut the matrices and made the types originally for his own use, first employing it for a book of poetry, *Two Singers*, by Charles Hanson Towne, that Goudy set and printed in his shop with the help of Peter Beilenson, who later established the Peter Pauper Press. Goudy's roman and italic designs were adapted for digital type by the P22 Type Foundry in Buffalo, New York. This book was designed and typeset by Richard Mathews at the University of Tampa Press. It has been printed on acid-free paper in support of the Green Press Initiative.

POETRY FROM THE UNIVERSITY OF TAMPA PRESS

Jordan Smith, *The Names of Things Are Leaving*

Jordan Smith, *The Light in the Film*

Lisa M. Steinman, *Carslaw's Sequences*

Marjorie Stelmach, *Bent upon Light*

Marjorie Stelmach, *A History of Disappearance*

Richard Terrill, *Coming Late to Rachmaninoff*

Richard Terrill, *Almost Dark*

Matt Yurdana, *Public Gestures*

* Denotes winner of the Tampa Review Prize for Poetry